Farmer Boy

Written By: Laura Ingalls Wilder

Student Study Guide

Published by: Memoria Press
www.memoriapress.com

ISBN: 978-1-61538-045-9

Contributing Editors: Leigh Lowe, Brenda Janke, Anne Parry, Brittany Mann
Cover Illustration by Starr Steinbach
Cover & Layout Design by Karah J. Force

Contents

Farmer Boy

Appendix 83

PREPARING TO READ:

REVIEW

- Orally review any previous vocabulary.
- Review the plot of the book as read so far.
- Periodically review the concepts of character, setting, and plot.

STUDY GUIDE PREVIEW

- Reading Notes:
    - Read aloud together
    - This section gives the student key characters, places, terms that are relevant to a particular time period, etc.
- Vocabulary:
    - Read aloud together so that students will recognize words when they come across them in their reading.
- Comprehension Questions:
    - Read through these questions with students to encourage purposeful reading.

READING:

- Student reads the chapter (or selection of the chapter for that lesson) independently or to the teacher (for younger students).
- For younger students, you can alternate between teacher-read and student-read passages. Model good reading skills. Encourage students to read expressively and smoothly. Teacher may occasionally take oral reading grades.
- While reading, mark each vocabulary word as you come across it.
- Have students take note in their study guide margin of pages where a comprehension question is answered.

AFTER READING:

VOCABULARY

- Look at each word within the context that it is used, and help your student come up with the best synonym that defines the word. (Make sure it is a synonym the student knows the meaning of.)
- Record the word's meaning in the students' study guides. (Use students' knowledge of Latin and other vocabulary to decipher meanings.)

COMPREHENSION QUESTIONS

- Older students can answer these questions independently, but younger students (2nd-4th) need to answer the questions orally, form a good sentence, and then write it down, using correct punctuation, capitalization, and spelling. (You may want to write the sentence down for the younger student after forming it orally, and then let the student copy it perfectly.)
- It is not necessary to write the answer to every question. Some may be better answered orally.
- Answering questions and composing answers is a valuable learning activity. Questions require students to think; writing a concise answer is a good composition exercise.

QUOTATIONS AND DISCUSSION QUESTIONS

- Use the Quotations and Discussion Questions section of each lesson as a guide to your oral discussion of the key concepts in the chapter that may not be covered in the comprehension questions.
- These talking points can take your oral discussion to a higher level than covered in the students' written work. Use this time as an opportunity to introduce higher-level thinking. You can introduce concepts the students may not be mature enough to fully understand yet but that would be beneficial for them to begin thinking about.
- A key to the Discussion Questions is in the back of the Teacher Guide.

ENRICHMENT

- The Enrichment activities include composition, copywork, dictation, research, mapping, drawing, poetry work, literary terms, and more.
- This section has a variety of activities in it, but the most valuable activity is composition. Your student should complete at least one composition assignment each week. Proof student's work and have student copy composition until grammatically perfect. Insist on clear, concise writing. For younger students, start with 2-3 sentences, and do the assignment together. The student can form good sentences orally as you write them down, and then the student copies them.
- These activities can be completed as time and interest allow. Do not feel you need to complete all of these activities. Choose the ones that you feel are the best use of your students' time.

UNIT REVIEW AND TESTS

- There is a unit review and a quiz or test following every few lessons (varies by individual guide).
- On the weeks that have these reviews and tests, you may want to do the review early in the week, and then drill it orally a couple of times before giving the test at the end of the week.
- A final comprehensive test is also included.

Reading Notes

waist the upper part of a garment, extending from the shoulders to the waistline
moccasins soft leather slippers
primer an elementary textbook for teaching children to read
jeering mocking; taunting

Vocabulary

1. a little boy **trudged** to school ______
2. Five big boys were **scuffling** in the deep snow by the path. ______
3. They **boasted** that no teacher could finish the winter term ______
4. Mr. Corse **rapped** on his desk with his ruler ______
5. No whispering was permitted in school, and no **fidgeting**. ______

Comprehension Questions

1. Give the names and ages of the four Wilder children. ______
2. Briefly describe Eliza Jane. ______
3. Why does Almanzo have to be the one to carry the dinner-pail to school? ______
4. Who is the teacher and why is he staying with the Wilder family at their home? ______
5. Find where Mr. Corse is described and list three characteristics that describe him. ______
6. In what way are students punished for not knowing their lessons? ______

Quotations

No whispering was permitted in school, and no fidgeting. Everyone must be perfectly still and keep his eyes fixed on his lesson. Almanzo and Miles held up their primers and tried not to swing their legs. Their legs grew so tired that they ached, dangling from the edge of the seat.

But Mr. Corse never beat a little boy's hand with his ruler. When Almanzo could not spell a word, Mr. Corse said: "Stay in at recess and learn it."

Discussion Questions

1. *Find the title page of the book, then turn the page to see publishing information. In what year did Laura Ingalls Wilder write *Farmer Boy*? Based on this knowledge and the first paragraph of the chapter, figure out the year in which the story is set. Where does the story take place?
2. Locate New York state on a U.S. map. What would the weather be like in that part of the country?
3. Why does Mr. Corse give the Hardscrabble boys another chance after they are tardy?
4. Explain the seating arrangement in the classroom. What do you think is the purpose of this arrangement?

*Discussion questions that have a * are NECESSARY to discuss with students, as they may appear on a test and are generally important in understanding the full flavor of the story.

Enrichment

Focus Passage: Copy the second paragraph beginning on page 1 ("Down a long road … nine years old"). Spelling, punctuation, and capitalization should be perfect.

____

____

____

____

____

____

____

____

____

____

____

Reading Notes

eave	the part of a roof that extends out past the wall
fringe	a decorative border or edging of hanging threads attached to a band
haymow	the part of a barn where hay or straw is stored
hoopskirt	a long full skirt belled out with a series of connected circular supports

Vocabulary

1. The wise, sedate work-horses **placidly** munched hay. ______________________
2. But the colts ran about excited, on their **gangling** legs ______________________
3. a plate of **quivering** headcheese ______________________
4. Almanzo ate the sweet, **mellow** baked beans. ______________________
5. He **demolished** a tall heap of pale mashed turnips ______________________

Comprehension Questions

1. What chores does Almanzo do after school? How are they different from the chores his sisters does? ______________________
____
____
____
2. Contrast the old work-horses with the young colts. ______________________
____
____
3. Describe Mother. ______________________
____
4. Who gets served a plate of food first? Who gets served last? Why? ______________________
____
____
5. Why can't Almanzo speak at the table? ______________________
____

Quotations

Father was an important man. He had a good farm. He drove the best horses in that country. His word was as good as his bond, and every year he put money in the bank. When Father drove into Malone, all the townspeople spoke to him respectfully.

The cold was cruel. The night was black and still, and the stars were tiny sparkles in the sky. Almanzo was glad to get into the big kitchen, warm with fire and candle-light. He was very hungry.

Discussion Questions

1. *The first quote above describes Father. According to it and other statements in the chapter, what kind of a man is he? What does the author mean by saying, "His word was as good as his bond"? From this chapter, how can you tell he is a good father to his children?
2. *Why doesn't Father trust Almanzo around the colts? What does he fear will happen, and how does Almanzo feel about this?
3. In the second quote above, the cold is described as being cruel. What does that mean? How does that phrase help you understand how Almanzo is feeling at that moment?

Enrichment

The author describes the Wilders' barnyard in great detail. When a story includes considerable descriptions like these, it is helpful to draw a picture of what it might look like. It can then be used later for reference and clarity.

Draw a simple map of the Wilder barnyard below. Label each barn and what it is used for. *(Suggestion: begin with a small compass star in a corner. Use a pencil so you can erase if necessary.)*

Reading Notes

embroidery	a design sewn on cloth as a decoration
dampers	a movable plate in a fireplace used to regulate the draft
bureau	a piece of furniture; dresser

Vocabulary

1. Mother and the girls washed the dishes and swept the **pantry** ______________________
2. Mother **banked** the kitchen fire with ashes for the night______________________
3. he broke the **charred** logs into a shimmering bed of coals. ______________________
4. He ran **clattering** upstairs.______________________
5. Father was **rousing** up the young cattle. ______________________

Comprehension Questions

1. What are the Wilder family bedtime snacks? What do they do for entertainment at night? ________

   ____

   ____

   ____

   ____

2. What does popcorn make Almanzo think of?______________________

   ____

   ____

3. Why does father get up at night to exercise the young cattle? ______________________

   ____

   ____

   ____

4. Why does Almanzo dread going to school?______________________

   ____

   ____

Quotations

They all settled down cosily by the big stove in the dining-room wall. … Mother knitted and rocked in her high-backed rocking-chair. Father carefully scraped a new ax-handle with a bit of broken glass. Royal carved a chain of tiny links from a smooth stick of pine, and Alice sat on her hassock, doing her woolwork embroidery. And they all ate popcorn and apples, and drank sweet cider, except Eliza Jane. Eliza Jane read aloud the news in the New York weekly paper. Almanzo sat on a footstool by the stove … He thought about popcorn.

Discussion Questions

1. What chores does the family do immediately after supper?
2. Find the pages that describe the Wilders' breakfast. What do they eat? Why do you think Mother cooks so much variety for this meal?

Enrichment

Learn More: The words below are unique to the setting of *Farmer Boy.*

Find the meaning of the words or phrases to learn more about how the Wilders lived. Write a short definition that explains or describes each.

parlor: ______________________________

dinner-pail: ______________________________

pannikin: ______________________________

tallow: ______________________________

cellar: ______________________________

hassock: ______________________________

goose-feather bed: ______________________________

headcheese: ______________________________

Reading Notes

trustees	members of a board elected to make important decisions for an organization
lick	to fight and defeat
bested	defeated

Vocabulary

1. they all grinned **impudently** at Mr. Corse. ____________________
2. they went in **soberly** and **soberly** sat down. ____________________
3. The big boys came … **jostling** one another. ____________________
4. Big Bill Ritchie **swaggered** in. ____________________
5. He **blubbered** and begged. ____________________

Comprehension Questions

1. Describe Mr. Ritchie. Why is he proud of his son, Big Bill Ritchie? ____________________
2. Why don't the students know their lessons on this day? ____________________
3. What makes Big Bill's gang change their attitude? ____________________
4. Describe the surprising events that occur at school. ____________________
5. What news does Almanzo overhear while his father and Mr. Corse are talking? ____________________

Quotations

"That's his business. When a man undertakes a job, he has to stick to it till he finishes it. If Corse is the man I think he is, he'd thank nobody for interfering."

Who said this? About whom? ______________________________

Discussion Questions

1. *In the quote above, what is Father saying about Mr. Corse?
2. Why does Mr. Corse focus on Big Bill instead of dealing with any of the other big boys first?
3. What virtues does Mr. Corse display in the way he disciplines Big Bill?

Enrichment

Focus Passage: Look at the last full paragraph on page 40, beginning with "That's his business ..." Copy the entire paragraph *directly* from the book. Spelling, punctuation, and capitalization should be perfect.

____

____

____

____

____

____

____

Reading Notes

yoke	a crossbar with two U-shaped pieces that encircle the necks of a pair of animals working together
"break" the calves	to train to obey; to tame
shingle	a thin, oblong piece of material, such as wood, laid in overlapping rows to cover the roof of a building
treadle	a pedal or lever operated by the foot
stanchion	a framework of vertical bars, used to secure cattle in a stall

Vocabulary

1. Their little red sides were **sleek** and silky ______________________
2. they stared **innocently** at him. ______________________
3. but of course he could not **contradict** Father. ______________________
4. Calves will get **sullen** and stop minding you ______________________
5. and **daintily** pawed with their slender legs and little hoofs ______________________

Comprehension Questions

1. Why does Almanzo not have to go to school on his birthday? ______________________

____

____

2. What is Almanzo's first birthday present? ______________________

____

3. Why does Almanzo feel as if the whole morning has gone by in only a moment? ______________________

____

____

4. Why is Almanzo allowed to train his calves but not Father's colts? ______________________

____

____

5. How does Mother surprise Almanzo? ______________________

____

Quotations

"Well, son, I'll leave you to figure it out." And he went into the barn.

Who said this? ______________________________ To whom? ______________________________

"Whose sled is that, Father? Is it—it isn't for me?" Mother laughed and Father twinkled his eyes and asked, "Do you know any other nine-year-old that wants it?"

Discussion Questions

1. *Read the first quote above. The book says Almanzo feels he is now old enough to do important things by himself. Why? Why do you think Father stops helping him and goes into the barn?
2. Explain how Almanzo teaches Star and Bright to understand "Giddap" and "Whoa."
3. While Almanzo is watching Mother work, she tells him she is making a suit for Royal that he will need next winter. Why will it take her so long to make this suit?
4. Compare and contrast Almanzo's birthday with your own birthday celebration.

Enrichment

Focus Passage: Look at the fifth paragraph on page 50 beginning with "Almanzo did not …" Copy the entire paragraph *directly* from the book. Spelling, punctuation, and capitalization should be perfect.

____

____

____

____

____

____

____

____

____

____

____

____

Reading Notes

bobsled	a long sled made of two shorter sleds joined together, one behind the other
plaid	cloth with a checked pattern
laprobe	a blanket or fur piece used to cover the lap, legs, and feet

Vocabulary

1. The horses trotted **briskly** ______________________________
2. A sharp wind blew there, driving **wisps** of snow before it. ______________________________
3. He felt himself falling **headlong** into the dark water. ______________________________
4. leaving them to fill every **crevice** tightly with sawdust ______________________________
5. and handed him the pitcher of sweetened cream **speckled** with nutmeg. ______________________________

Comprehension Questions

1. What type of weather was perfect for cutting ice? Why? ______________________________

____

____

2. Who are Lazy John and French Joe? Compare them to the Wilder family. ______________________________

____

____

____

____

3. Describe what happens when Almanzo gets too close to the edge of the hole. ______________________________

____

____

4. How do the Wilders keep the ice frozen even in the summer months? ______________________________

____

____

5. How do Almanzo and Royal distract themselves until dinnertime? ______________________________

____

Quotations

"You flipped that penny yet?" Everybody laughed but Almanzo. He did not know the joke.

Who said this? ______________________ To whom? ______________________

French Joe grabbed him just in time. He heard a shout and felt a rough hand jerk him by one leg, he felt a terrific crash, and then he was lying on his stomach on the good, solid ice. He got up on his feet. Father was coming, running.

Discussion Questions

1. Read the first quote. What is the punchline of the "flip a penny" joke? Why is it about Irishmen, not Frenchmen?
2. What would have happened if Almanzo had actually fallen in the ice?
3. Why do you think sawdust is used to cover the top layer of ice and to fill the cracks?
4. How do the Wilders use the ice they store in the summer months?

Enrichment

Sequencing: Describe the process of cutting ice and filling the ice house.Your sentences should be organized to show the correct order of the tasks. Be sure to write in complete sentences.

1. ____

____

2. ____

____

3. ____

____

4. ____

____

5. ____

____

6. ____

____

Reading Notes

new-fangled	new type or style
muffler	a heavy scarf worn around the neck
Comanches	a Native American people formerly living in the southern Great Plains
rye'n'injun dough	a combination of rye and corn dough ("injun" - Indian)
drawers	thermal underwear pants

Vocabulary

1. Royal chopped at it, and when his **hatchet** went through ____________________
2. An **avalanche** of ice came down with a splintering crash. ____________________
3. The noise was **immense**. ____________________
4. Such a **racket** I never heard! ____________________
5. pouring **scrolls** of molasses over all. ____________________

Comprehension Questions

1. What does Almanzo like best about Saturdays? What does he like least? ____________________

   ____
2. Why does Mother prepare Sunday dinner on Saturday night? ____________________

   ____
3. What is the Saturday-night feeling? ____________________

   ____
4. How does Mother determine whether or not Almanzo is clean? Why does she need to check him?

   ____

   ____

   ____
5. Why do the Wilders bathe only once a week on Saturday night? ____________________

   ____

   ____

   ____

Quotations

Almanzo liked baking-day. But he didn't like Saturday night. On Saturday night there was no cosy evening by the heater, with apples, popcorn, and cider. Saturday night was bath night.

He felt very clean and good, and his skin felt sleek in the fresh, warm clothes. It was the Saturday-night feeling.

Who is this referring to? ______________________________

Discussion Questions

1. How does Mother make doughnuts? What is special about her doughnuts?
2. The Wilders' bath procedure is involved. What other chores were more difficult then?
3. What bedtime clothing does Almanzo put on after his bath? Why must he dress so warmly?

Enrichment

Focus Passage: Reread the first quote above, then copy it on the lines below. Spelling, punctuation, and capitalization should be perfect.

Reading Notes

sleigh	a light vehicle mounted on runners for use on snow or ice, drawn by a horse
calico	light-weight, printed cotton fabric
basque	a woman's close-fitting bodice

Vocabulary

1. Mother … buttered it **lavishly** ______
2. Oh dear me, my ribbons are **mussed**. ______
3. Then they all walked **sedately** into the church. ______
4. Father allowed him to brush and **currycomb** … the horses ______
5. The whole afternoon they sat in the **drowsy** warm dining-room. ______

Comprehension Questions

1. What are the three grades of cloth mentioned? Who wears each type? ______
2. Why do the Wilders travel to Malone? How far away is Malone? ______
3. Where does Almanzo's cousin Frank live? Why? ______
4. How does the Wilder family always spend their Sunday afternoons? Why? ______
5. Why is Almanzo glad to do the chores Sunday evening? ______

Quotations

Mother always flew. Her feet went pattering, her hands moved so fast you could hardly watch them. She never sat down in the daytime, except at her spinning-wheel or loom ... But on Sunday morning she made everybody else hurry, too.

But Almanzo just sat. He had to. He was not allowed to do anything else, for Sunday was not a day for working or playing. It was a day for going to church and for sitting still.

Discussion Questions

1. "Every man who belonged to the church paid rent for a shed, according to his means, and Father had the best one." What does the phrase "according to his means" mean? What does this say about Father?
2. *Farmer Boy* includes many detailed descriptions of food. Why do you think this is?
3. What are Almanzo's thoughts about his cousin Frank's "store-boughten" cap? Based on what Royal says, how does Almanzo know he wants a cap like that too?
4. Consider the way in which the Wilders traveled. Contrast the differences between their means of travel and how you travel.

Enrichment

Focus Passage: Copy from the second paragraph on page 94 beginning with "But Almanzo just sat ..." through the last paragraph of the chapter, ending with "... time to do the chores." Since you are beginning your copying in the middle of a paragraph, don't worry about indenting this time. Spelling, punctuation, and capitalization should be perfect.

Reading Notes

whiplash a flexible whip used to train oxen
auger a hand tool used to drill holes in wood or ice
fraidy-cat slang for a timid or fearful person

Vocabulary

1. They kicked up their heels and ran **bawling** around the barnyard____________________
2. When the calves feel the **heft,** they're liable to run away.____________________
3. When the calves feel the heft, they're **liable** to run away. ____________________
4. He spit it out, and **wallowed**, scrambled up. ____________________
5. The yoke was crooked and their necks were **askew** in the bows. ____________________

Comprehension Questions

1. How does Almanzo teach Star and Bright to turn right and left? ____________________
2. Why does Almanzo tell Father about his patience while training the oxen? ____________________
3. Who are the French boys? Who are their fathers? ____________________
4. What is Almanzo's splendid idea concerning his calves? ____________________
5. What does Almanzo forget to teach Star and Bright? ____________________

Eliza Jane was mortified when Father drank from a saucer. Mother was angry and took her hands out of&the dishpan and asked eliza Jane where sawcers came from.

Eliza Jane opened and shut her

Quotations

He knew you could never teach an animal anything if you struck it, or even shouted at it angrily. He must always be gentle, and quiet, and patient, even when they made mistakes. Star and Bright must like him and trust him and know he would never hurt them, for if they were once afraid of him they would never be good, willing, hard-working oxen.

"I guess I know how to handle my own calves."

Who said this? ________________________________

Discussion Questions

1. Based on the first quote above, why does Almanzo not whip Star and Bright even when they are not obeying?
2. Read the second quote. Why does Almanzo say this? Judging from the outcome of his "splendid idea," do you agree with this statement? Why or why not?

Enrichment

Focus Passage: Copy the last paragraph on page 98 ("He knew you …") through the top of page 99 to the end of the paragraph ("… hard-working oxen."). Spelling, punctuation, and capitalization should be perfect.

Reading Notes

caldron a large kettle used for boiling
fetch to go after something and bring it back

Vocabulary

1. The days were growing longer, but the cold was more **intense**. ____________________
2. In every maple tree Father had **bored** a small hole____________________
3. gushing out their **aromatic** juice. ____________________
4. the snow was **pitted** with water falling from the icicles____________________
5. "That's pretty good," Mother said, **beaming**. ____________________

Comprehension Questions

1. What does Almanzo love about being in the frozen wild woods?____________________

2. Who comes to buy the potatoes? How many bushels are sold? For how much money? ________

3. How do Almanzo and Alice make the work of loading the potatoes into baskets more fun? ______

4. List the Wilders' spring-cleaning chores.____________________

Quotations

"When the days begin to lengthen, the cold begins to strengthen."

At noon all the sap was boiling in the caldron. Father opened the lunch-pail, and Almanzo sat on the log beside him. They ate and talked. Their feet were stretched out to the fire, and a pile of logs was at their backs. All around them were snow and ice and wild woods, but they were snug and cosy.

Discussion Questions

1. Explain the first quote above.
2. Explain how maple syrup and maple sugar are made.

Enrichment

Focus Passage: Copy the second full paragraph on page 111 beginning with "At noon …" Spelling, punctuation, and capitalization should be perfect.

Elements of Literature

Writing sentences about the story.

Character: Character means who is in the story.

1. List the major characters in *Farmer Boy.* ____________________

   ____

2. List the minor characters in *Farmer Boy*. ____________________

   ____

Setting: Setting means the time and place in which the story happens.

1. Describe the general setting of *Farmer Boy.* ____________________

   ____

2. List the seasons that the Wilders have experienced thus far. ____________________

   ____

Plot: Plot means action or what happens in the story.

Write out details about your favorite chapter in *Farmer Boy* so far. Use complete sentences.

____

Drawing Page

Illustrate your favorite chapter from the previous page.

Quiz 1 Review

Vocabulary

Write the letter of the vocabulary word on the line in front of its definition.

1. _______ bragged
2. _______ extreme
3. _______ destroyed
4. _______ scented
5. _______ to speak against
6. _______ quickly; with spirit
7. _______ walked with heavy feet
8. _______ weight
9. _______ waking
10. _______ small short-handled ax
11. _______ smooth; slick
12. _______ sleepy
13. _______ wrestling
14. _______ loud noise; clamor
15. _______ moody
16. _______ area for food storage
17. _______ seriously
18. _______ crack
19. _______ calmly, peacefully
20. _______ drilled
21. _______ partially burned
22. _______ bent to one side
23. _______ trembling
24. _______ generously; extravagantly
25. _______ disrespectfully

a. contradict
b. charred
c. racket
d. demolished
e. soberly
f. drowsy
g. pantry
h. askew
i. boasted
j. intense
k. crevice
l. quivering
m. aromatic
n. impudently
o. heft
p. trudged
q. lavishly
r. rousing
s. sullen
t. bored
u. scuffling
v. sleek
w. briskly
x. placidly
y. hatchet

Short Answer

Answer the following questions in complete sentences.

1. What is the setting of *Farmer Boy*? Where and in what year does it take place? ____________

2. Briefly describe the "surprise" that occurs at school involving Big Bill's gang and Mr. Corse. ____________

3. How do the Wilders keep the ice frozen even in the hot summer months? ____________

4. What is Almanzo's "splendid" idea concerning his calves, and why does it go wrong? ____________

5. Why doesn't Father trust Almanzo around the colts? What does he fear will happen? ____________

Reading Notes

harrow	a farm machine with sharp teeth used to break up and level plowed ground; it is also used as a verb to describe the process of preparing the soil for planting
dinner-horn	a simple wind instrument used to call field workers home for a meal
seed corn	kernels of corn used for planting

Vocabulary

1. the sun was rising beyond the **dewy** meadows ______
2. They dribbled the carrot seeds into the **furrows** ______
3. All the soil must be made **mellow** and fine and smooth. ______
4. **Hustle** along there, son ______
5. Almanzo … went up and down the long field, **straddling** the little furrows. ______

______

Comprehension Questions

1. The experienced work horses know exactly what to do in the fields. Why would Almanzo have enjoyed driving them more if this weren't the case? ______

______

______

2. Why do the farmers have to hurry to plant their good seeds? ______

______

______

______

3. What are the three fields of grain Father sows? What are they used for? ______

______

______

______

4. Explain the connection between ash leaves, squirrel ears, and corn planting. ______

______

Quotations

Almanzo was a little soldier in this great battle. From dawn to dark he worked, from dark to dawn he slept, then he was up again and working.

But Almanzo had never planted corn before. He did not handle the hoe so well. He had to trot two steps where Royal or Father took one … But he knew he would plant corn as fast as anybody, when his legs were longer.

Discussion Questions

1. The third paragraph of this chapter describes the work horses. Explain the phrase "wise, sober mares."
2. The first quote above describes Almanzo as a soldier in a battle. What is the battle, and in what way is he like a soldier in this battle?
3. Describe how the potatoes are planted.

Enrichment

Composition: Reread the last paragraph on page 128, beginning with "The seeds were too small …" In three to five sentences, retell the story of the lazy boy in your own words. Be sure to include the consequence of his actions.

Reading Notes

colander	a bowl-shaped kitchen utensil with holes for draining off liquids
solder	to join metal objects using heated metal

Vocabulary

1. the young horses … **whinnied** to the big white horse. ____________________
2. Nick Brown, the tin-**peddler**, was a jolly, fat man ____________________
3. Mother was a good, **shrewd** trader. ____________________
4. The big white horse stepped out **eagerly** ____________________
5. The red cart went past the house and **lurched** into the road ____________________

Comprehension Questions

1. Who is Nick Brown? Why are the Wilders eager to see him? ____________________

____

____

____

2. Describe some of the wares the peddler brings. ____________________

____

____

____

3. Where does the peddler get the tin ware he sells? ____________________

____

4. What does Mother use instead of money to trade with the peddler? ____________________

____

5. Describe the way Mother and Mr. Brown bargain. Who wins? ____________________

____

____

____

Quotations

"I'll tell story for story and sing song for song, as long as you'll bring men up against me, and when they're all done, I'll tell the last story and sing the last song."

Who said this? ______________________________

For a long time they talked and argued. … For every pile of rags that Nick Brown added to the big pile, Mother asked more tinware than he wanted to trade her. They were both having a good time, joking and laughing and trading.

Discussion Questions

1. Think back to the types of wares the peddler brings. Does your family use any of these items? Are there items he sells that we don't use at all anymore?
2. What would the life of a peddler be like? Would it be an adventure or a chore? Why?
3. What kinds of people might a peddler meet on his journeys?

Enrichment

Literary Terms:
Alliteration is the intentional repetition of a beginning consonant sound. An example is shown below:

Mr. Brown ... rubbed him down with clean cloths.

In the sentences below, underline the beginning consonant sounds that are repeated.

1. Almanzo and Royal put on their coats and caps and mufflers and mittens.
2. He blubbered and begged.
3. He was a big, rough man with a loud voice and a loud laugh.
4. Ten stacks of pancakes rose in tall towers.
5. Almanzo walked whistling behind his team.
6. Alice and Almanzo carried pails full of pieces of potato.
7. There were tin horns, tin whistles, toy tin dishes and patty-pans.
8. Every piece was good thick tin, well made and solidly soldered.
9. Mother was short and plump and pretty.
10. The cold was cruel.

Reading Notes

"full of ginger"	lively; energetic
sha'n't / 'twa'n't	slang contractions for "shall not" and "it was not"
Providence	a term referring to God

Vocabulary

1. Then there were the **mangers** and stalls to clean ____________________
2. Something or somebody's **prowling** round this house! ____________________
3. they all heard a **stealthy** sound ____________________
4. she heard a low, **savage** growl. ____________________
5. I made **inquiry**, and he was at the hotel ____________________

Comprehension Questions

1. Describe the appearance of the horse-buyer. ____________________
2. What does his appearance lead you to predict about his personality? ____________________
3. Why is supper time not as cheerful as usual on the night the horses are sold? ____________________
4. Describe the strange dog. How does he help the Wilder family? ____________________
5. What does Father learn when he arrives in Malone? ____________________

Quotations

Almanzo knew that in the whole world there was nothing so beautiful, so fascinating, as beautiful horses. When he thought that it would be years and years before he could have a little colt to teach and take care of, he could hardly bear it.

"Broken to drive double or single. They're high-spirited, full of ginger, and gentle as kittens. A lady can drive them."

Who said this? ______________________ About what? ______________________

Discussion Questions

1. *In what small way does Father acknowledge that Almanzo is becoming more trustworthy around the young horses?
2. How is Father's bargaining with the horse-buyer similar to Mother's trading for tin-ware?
3. Why do you think Mother hears the noise in the middle of the night, but Father sleeps soundly?

Enrichment

Focus Passage: Copy the third paragraph on page 142, beginning with "Almanzo knew that …" Spelling, punctuation, and capitalization should be perfect.

Reading Notes

bleating	the crying of a sheep
fleece	the wool coat of a sheep
Merinos	a breed of sheep with long, fine wool

Vocabulary

1. It was time to **shear** sheep. ____________________
2. they **boosted** it up the bank ____________________
3. they scattered up the **slope** ____________________
4. He didn't mean to **idle** ____________________
5. Father spoke to him **sternly**. ____________________

Comprehension Questions

1. Sheep washing is like an assembly line. What is each person's job? ____________________

2. In what way are Father's sheep special? How does that make shearing them a greater challenge?

3. What causes Almanzo to fall behind in his work? ____________________

4. What is the trick Almanzo plays on John? ____________________

Quotations

Washing sheep was fun for everybody but the sheep. The men splashed and shouted and laughed in the water, and the boys ran and shouted in the pasture. The sun was warm on their backs and the grass was cool under bare feet, and all their laughter was small in the wide, pleasant stillness of the green fields and meadows.

"He laughs best who laughs last!"

Who said this? ______________________ To whom? ______________________

Discussion Questions

1. Why do the men wash the sheep in the river instead of in tubs? Why are they washed before shearing instead of afterwards?
2. Why do you think Father laughs and says Almanzo can't keep up with the others after he has just sternly told him to do so? Do his words have the desired effect?
3. Why does Father think Almanzo's joke on Lazy John is so funny?
4. Explain why sheep are so important to the Wilder family.

Enrichment

Composition: Sheep shearing is complex work. Describe the steps in their correct order. Write complete sentences, using words like **first, next, then,** and **finally**.

Reading Notes

card / carding machine	the process and/or the implement used to brush, clean, and disentangle the short fibers of wool
lye	a strong solution obtained from filtering water through wood ashes; used in soap-making
ewes	female sheep

Vocabulary

1. Only small children went to the spring **term** of school ______
2. He watched the moon **anxiously** ______
3. No one had ever **taken such pains** with carrots as he did ______
4. Two **acres** of corn Almanzo hoed ______
5. right up to their **frail** lavender blossoms. ______

Comprehension Questions

1. What are some of nature's signs that something is going wrong with springtime? ______
2. Why does Almanzo anxiously await the dark of the moon? ______
3. What is Almanzo trying to avoid and how does he avoid it? ______
4. How are Father's fears justified about the slow-growing corn? ______
5. How do the Wilders save most of the corn crop? Why do they lose the last quarter acre? ______

Quotations

Father and Mother and Royal and Eliza Jane and Alice and Almanzo filled their pails with water, and they all went to work, as fast as they could.

What was this work? ______________________________

Almanzo ran to fill his pail; he ran back. He ran down the rows, splashing water on the hills of corn. His shoulders ached and his arm ached and there was a pain in his side. The soft earth hung on to his feet. He was terribly hungry. But every splash of water saved a hill of corn.

Discussion Questions

1. Explain Mother's process for soap-making.
2. What is meant by the sentence "The sun was coming to kill the corn"?
3. Reread the two quotes above. Why do you think the Wilders are able to save most of the corn even though there are thousands of hills of it and they don't start working until the middle of the night? Why is it so important to them to save it?

Enrichment

Dictation: Listen carefully as your teacher reads aloud. As she reads, write down what you hear. Pay close attention to spelling, capitalization and punctuation. When finished, compare your paragraph to the book, and circle any errors.

____

____

____

____

____

____

____

____

____

____

____

Reading Notes

parasol	light-weight umbrella used for shielding from the sun
Congressman	a member of Congress; a political figure
Declaration of Independence	the document that announced the independence of the American colonies from the British Empire
Redcoat	a British soldier serving during the American Revolution
musket	type of gun
Revolution	refers to the American Revolution

Vocabulary

1. They passed gray … and **dappled**-gray horses. ______________________
2. Almanzo felt solemn and very **proud**. ______________________
3. The music was so **gay**… ______________________
4. I'd just as **lief** ask him if I wanted to. ______________________
5. He was **faint-hearted**, but he had to go. ______________________

Comprehension Questions

1. Once they arrive in Malone, why does Almanzo stay with Father instead of hurrying off like the rest of the family? ______________________

   ____
2. How does Frank get Almanzo to ask for the nickel? ______________________

   ____
3. Why does Father ask Almanzo about potatoes? What does this have to do with the half-dollar?

   ____

   ____

   ____

   ____
4. How does Almanzo decide to spend his half-dollar? ______________________

   ____

Quotations

All the country had a holiday air. Nobody was working in the fields, and along the road the people in their Sunday clothes were driving to town.

"It was farmers that took all that country and made it America. … But we were farmers, son; we wanted the land. It was farmers that went over the mountains, and cleared the land, and settled it, and farmed it, and hung on to their farms."

Who said this? ________________________________

Discussion Questions

1. Explain how Independence Day is celebrated in the town of Malone. What are the main events during the celebration?
2. How do Frank and Mr. Paddock respond similarly in this chapter?
3. Using the second quote above, explain Father's earlier statement: "It was axes and plows that made this country."

Enrichment

Literary Terms:
Onomatopoeia occurs when a word imitates a sound or sounds like what it describes. For example:

pop *hiss* *crack* *sizzle*

In each sentence below, underline words that are examples of onomatopoeia.

1. The fifes tooted and the flutes shrilled.
2. The drummer beat rat-a-tat-tat and rub-a-dub-dub on the drum.
3. The Stars and Stripes fluttered and flapped.
4. Then came buglers blowing and fifers tootling.
5. Then — BOOM!
6. Grandmother told us to hush.
7. Several small logs in the fire crackled at once.
8. We saw bees buzz wildly around their heads.
9. The whole hive murmured.
10. Leaves rustled as the squirrel moved through them.

Reading Notes

laid by	set aside for future use
bridles / harness	gear fitted on a horse, used to guide it during farm labor
"tan your jacket"	to be disciplined with a switch; a severe spanking

Vocabulary

1. they carefully made a little **slit** on the underside of the vine. ____________________
2. Then he put a candle **wick** in the milk ____________________
3. he wouldn't teach them to jump, or **balk** ____________________
4. I did lay out to **cultivate** the carrots and mend fence. ____________________
5. Almanzo … watched the raindrops **dimpling** the water. ____________________

Comprehension Questions

1. Why does Almanzo try to eat so much? ____________________

____

____

2. Who is Starlight? What does Father say when Almanzo tries to touch him? ____________________

____

____

____

3. Why doesn't Almanzo ask his father about fishing? ____________________

____

____

4. What does Almanzo have to do on rainy days? Why? ____________________

____

____

____

____

Quotations

Nothing ever smelled so good as the rain on clover. Nothing ever felt so good as raindrops on Almanzo's face, and the wet grass swishing around his legs. Nothing ever sounded so pleasant as the drops pattering on the bushes along Trout River, and the rush of the water over the rocks.

To what does this refer? ____________________

"All work and no play makes Jack a dull boy. Tomorrow we'll go berrying."

Who said this? ____________________

Discussion Questions

1. *What does Father teach Almanzo about growing pumpkins? Explain the process.
2. Explain the second quote above.
3. Describe the family berrying excursion and Almanzo's surprise encounter.

Enrichment

Focus Passage: Copy the last four paragraphs in the chapter (page 202) beginning with "It's time Mother and I ..." Spelling, punctuation, and capitalization should be perfect.

Reading Notes

rind	the tough outer skin of some fruits
yearling	an animal that is one year old
wabbling	means the same as "wobbling"; unsteady

Vocabulary

1. they **lugged** them one by one to the ice house ____________________
2. The air shimmered and **wavered** with heat ____________________
3. Even Alice was **horrified** because he had wasted candy ____________________
4. Goodness! don't **dawdle** so! ____________________
5. "I guess I was **aggravating**," she said. "But I didn't mean to be." ____________________

Comprehension Questions

1. How do the children initially feel after their parents leave? What do they do first? ____________________
2. Who is Lucy? What happens when Almanzo feeds her candy? ____________________
3. Why are the children in a frenzy on the last day before Mother and Father return? ____________________
4. What happens between Almanzo and Eliza Jane in the parlor? ____________________

Quotations

"Well, Mother told you to obey me. And I'm not going to waste melon rinds on any pig! I'm going to make watermelon-rind preserves."

Who said this? ____________________ To whom? ____________________

"I guess I was aggravating," she said. "But I didn't mean to be. You're the only little brother I've got."

Who said this? ____________________ To whom? ____________________

Discussion Questions

1. What does Almanzo do as soon as he thinks no one is watching him? What happens?
2. What do Alice and Almanzo do in the parlor? Why do they hide their activity from Eliza Jane?
3. How does Almanzo's guilty conscience punish him when the Webbs come to visit?
4. Based on the entire chapter and the quotes above, is Eliza Jane a good sister to Almanzo? Why or why not?

Enrichment

Literary Terms:
Similes are expressions that compare two different things using "like" or "as."

In each sentence, circle "like" or "as," and underline the things being compared.

1. The dark hung like a mist over the field.
2. Their white blossoms were like foam on the field.
3. Their nostrils fluttered when they breathed; their ears moved as swiftly as birds.
4. Clean sheep scattered up the slope, making the pasture look like a snowball bush in bloom.
5. Quick as black lightning the lash circled and struck and coiled again.
6. He oiled their curved hoofs, till they shone black as Mother's polished stove.
7. The shocks looked like little Indian wigwams.
8. They're high-spirited, full of ginger, and gentle as kittens.
9. Pork-pickle had a stinging smell that felt like a sneeze.
10. The little pig was as white as a lamb, and she liked Almanzo.

Reading Notes

scythe	a farm tool with a long, curved blade used for mowing or reaping
timothy	a type of grass, cultivated for use as hay
whetstone	a hard stone used to sharpen tools
bombazine	a dressy fabric made of silk and cotton

Vocabulary

1. the **plumed** timothy fell in great swathes. ____________________
2. and the plumed timothy fell in great **swathes**. ____________________
3. Now the men **whetted** their scythes ____________________
4. Everything must be saved, nothing wasted of all the summer's **bounty**. ____________________
5. Father and Royal could bind oats as fast as the **reapers** cut them. ____________________

Comprehension Questions

1. Explain what Mother's dinner horn means when it blows in mid-morning. ____________________
2. When the heavy pail of egg-nog threatens to spill, how does Almanzo solve the problem? What is his reasoning? ____________________
3. Give reasons why Almanzo likes summer haying-time. ____________________
4. What is the difference between sheaves and shocks? Why do the oats have to be shocked before dark? ____________________

Quotations

There was no rest and no play for anyone now. They all worked from candle-light to candle-light. … Everything must be saved, nothing wasted of all the summer's bounty.

Mother did not do any bargaining at all. She said, proudly; "My butter speaks for itself."

Discussion Questions

1. Explain Lazy John's words when he says, "That puts heart into a man!"
2. Name all the work that must be done during the early harvest time.
3. Describe the butter-buyer's visit. Why does Mother make a trip to town afterwards? Why is this unusual?

Enrichment

Poetry Connection: "The Hayloft" by Robert Louis Stevenson is a delightful poem of a child at play in a hayloft. Almanzo may have spent time in this same way.

Do the following:

1. Find the poem "The Hayloft" in the Appendix.
2. Read it through several times.
3. Discuss the meanings of the words, the aspects of poetry, and its message.
4. Copy it carefully and precisely.
5. Then memorize it, so that you may enjoy it in the future, whenever you wish.

Reading Notes

harvest moon	the full moon that occurs nearest the autumnal equinox
hogshead	a large barrel or cask with a capacity ranging from 63-140 gallons
poultice	a soft, moist pack of medicinal herbs, applied to a wound to aid in healing

Vocabulary

1. Alice put on her hood and **shawl**. ______________________________
2. cold wind blew **gritty** dust into Almanzo's eyes. ______________________________
3. Alice held out her **grubby** hands to warm them______________________________
4. It stuck on his face, **scalding hot.** ______________________________
5. "I guess it's your potato," he **snuffled**. ______________________________

Comprehension Questions

1. Explain why the perfect apples are picked, hauled, and stored very carefully. How are the imperfect apples used? ______________________________
____
____
____
2. Why is Father in a hurry to harvest potatoes? ______________________________
____
3. How can Almanzo usually tell the time of day while outdoors? Why doesn't this method work when they are digging potatoes? ______________________________
____
4. How does Almanzo get blistered? ______________________________
____
5. Why does Almanzo insist on sharing the remaining potato with Alice?______________________________
____
____

Quotations

"No, it's yours. It was my potato that exploded." … "This one's yours because you're hurt, and I'm not hungry, anyway not very hungry."

Who said this? ______________________ To whom? ________

All the harvest was in, now. Cellar and attic and the barns were stuffed to bursting. Plenty of food, and plenty of feed for all the stock, was stored away for the winter.

Discussion Questions

1. Which crops are stored in the cellar? in the barn? in the attic? How is each type of food used?
2. What does Mother mean when she says, "A miss is as good as a mile"?

Enrichment

Quotation Review: How good is your memory?

For each of the following quotations, write the name of the person who said it. Look up the answer in the book if you need help.

1. "I'll tell story for story and sing song for song …" ______________(Ch. 12)
2. "All right, two hundred it is. I'll lose money by it, but here you are." ______________(Ch. 13)
3. "It's work, son. That's what money is; it's hard work." ______________(Ch. 16)
4. "I guess I know how to handle my own calves." ______________(Ch. 9)
5. "This one's yours because you're hurt …" ______________(Ch. 20)
6. "When a man undertakes a job, he has to stick to it till he finishes it." ______________(Ch. 4)
7. "I dare you to ask him." ______________(Ch. 16)
8. "You mean to say we must keep all that money in the house overnight!" ______________(Ch. 13)
9. "Stay in at recess and learn it." ______________(Ch. 1)
10. "They're high-spirited, full of ginger, and gentle as kittens." ______________(Ch. 13)
11. "I guess I was aggravating. But I didn't mean it." ______________(Ch. 18)
12. "There's the fleece! I've got it upstairs and you haven't sheared it! I beat you! I beat you!"

    ______________(Ch. 14)

Elements of Literature

Character: Character means who is in the story.

Identify the characters new to *Farmer Boy* since Lesson 10.

Setting: Setting means the time and place in which the story happens.

1. Describe the Wilders' farm at the turn of the year.
2. Describe the Wilders' farm in the spring.
3. Describe the Wilders' farm in the summer.
4. Describe the Wilders' farm in the fall.

Plot: Plot means action or what happens in the story.

Write about your favorite story in Chapters 11-20 of *Farmer Boy*. Use complete sentences.

Drawing Page

Illustrate each season in the space provided below.

Turn of the Year

Spring

Summer

Fall

Quiz 2 Review

Vocabulary

Write the letter of the vocabulary word on the line in front of its definition.

1. _______ sandy	a. cultivate
2. _______ plowed rows	b. frail
3. _______ flickered or glimmered	c. furrows
4. _______ roll or pitch suddenly; jerked	d. swathes
5. _______ sections, rows	e. shrewd
6. _______ cowardly	f. balk
7. _______ crafty; clever	g. sternly
8. _______ to stop short and refuse to go on	h. gritty
9. _______ hot enough to burn	i. faint-hearted
10. _______ sly; secretive	j. hustle
11. _______ generous amount	k. whetted
12. _______ grading period; semester	l. shear
13. _______ to waste time; to be slow	m. dawdle
14. _______ walking with one foot on either side	n. lurched
15. _______ greatly annoying	o. bounty
16. _______ sharpened	p. stealthy
17. _______ cut wool from	q. slit
18. _______ hurry	r. straddling
19. _______ to prepare; to tend	s. wavered
20. _______ fragile	t. inquiry
21. _______ firmly; severely	u. aggravating
22. _______ spotted	v. term
23. _______ small cut	w. dappled
24. _______ traveling salesman	x. peddler
25. _______ question	y. scalding-hot

Quiz 2 Review

Short Answer

Answer the following questions in complete sentences.

1. In what small way does Father acknowledge that Almanzo is becoming more trustworthy around the young horses? ____

2. Sheep shearing is done as an assembly line. What is each person's job? ____________________

3. Briefly describe what Father teaches Almanzo about growing pumpkins. ____________________

4. What happens between Almanzo and Eliza Jane in the parlor? ____________________________

5. Explain why the perfect apples are picked, hauled, and stored very carefully. How are the imperfect apples used? ____

Reading Notes

thoroughbred a horse bred chiefly for racing
haunch the back, upper leg and thigh of an animal
sulky an open two-wheeled vehicle drawn by one horse, used in harness racing

Vocabulary

1. people were **clustered** like flies. ______
2. The ground there was **trodden** into deep dust by the crowd ______
3. Those long ears stood up above their long, **gaunt** faces ______
4. Father **pried** off the cover of one barrel ______
5. But I would rather get something more **substantial** for mine. ______

Comprehension Questions

1. What is the first thing Almanzo wants to see at the fair? ______
2. What makes Almanzo feel important and grown-up? ______
3. Describe the two black creatures Almanzo sees in the stall. What is a mule? ______
4. Why does Almanzo feel "cold and small and scared" after winning? What does he soon realize? ______
5. Why doesn't Almanzo enjoy the third day of the fair? ______

Quotations

"What's the good of a horse that can pull a barn? We don't want to pull a barn. A Morgan has muscle enough to pull a wagon, and he's fast enough to pull a buggy, too." … Almanzo felt important and grown-up, talking horses with Father.

Who said this? ________________________________ About what? ________________________________

Then he knew he was telling a lie. Father was hearing him tell a lie. He looked up at Mr. Paddock and said: "I raised it on milk. It's a milk-fed pumpkin. Is—is that all right?"

Who said this? ________________________________

Discussion Questions

1. *Why does the county fair take place after all the crops are harvested?
2. Explain what Father means when he says: "Never bet your money on another man's game."
3. Describe the horse race. Why doesn't Father believe in betting on a winner?

Enrichment

Focus Passage: Copy the sixth paragraph on page 271 ("Father's hand clapped …"). Spelling, punctuation, and capitalization should be perfect. Copy the quotation marks carefully as well.

____

____

____

____

____

____

____

____

____

____

____

____

Reading Notes

twilight	the diffused light in the sky during early morning or evening when the sun is below the horizon
Indian summer	a period of mild weather occurring in late autumn

Vocabulary

1. Alice put on her **cloak** and hood ______________________
2. **delicate** bare limbs of the beeches. ______________________
3. Then he and Alice **trampled** down leaves again ______________________
4. **heaved** it out and laid it on boards. ______________________
5. [The tubes] … **tapered** to a point at the bottom ______________________

Comprehension Questions

1. Why does bitter cold mean it is butchering-time? ______________________
2. What are some of the tasks Father does around the farm to prepare for winter? ______________________
3. What does Father do with the beef hide? ______________________
4. How are Lazy John and French Joe paid for their labor? ______________________
5. What is the connection between pork fat, beef fat, tallow, and lard? ______________________

Quotations

Before they had finished, Lazy John and French Joe had come, and there was time to snatch only a bite of breakfast. Five hogs and a yearling beef were to be killed that day.

All this time he was grinding sausagemeat. He poked thousands of pieces of meat into the grinder and turned the handle round and round, for hours and hours. He was glad when that was finished.

To whom does this refer? ____________________________

Discussion Questions

1. What is "poor man's fertilizer"? Why is snow plowed into unfrozen ground valuable?
2. How are the Wilders like the squirrels that are busy storing nuts for the winter?
3. Explain how butchering is done.
4. What is headcheese? What is mincemeat? Use the book to find your answers.

Enrichment

Interpreting a Passage: The Wilders make candles in a way that is unfamiliar to most people today. Learning about ways that are unfamiliar to us always increases our knowledge.

Read the paragraphs about candle-making, beginning from the top of page 283 to the end of the chapter. Then, list the seven steps of candle-making that the book describes.

1. ____

____

2. ____
3. ____

____

4. ____
5. ____
6. ____

____

7. ____

____

Reading Notes

cobbler	one who mends or makes boots or shoes
indigo	a blue dye obtained from plants
carpet-bag	a traveling bag made of carpet fabric
tanned hides	chemically treated animal skins converted into leather

Vocabulary

1. Mother's **shears** went snickety-snick through the … cloth she had woven. ____________
2. Almanzo helped Father **husk** corn. ____________
3. She told Almanzo all about her lessons in music and **deportment** ____________
4. she was **mortified** because Father drank tea from his saucer. ____________
5. if you **drudge** all your days on a farm ____________

Comprehension Questions

1. Describe the cobbler. Why is he three weeks late? Why is Mother upset? ____________

   ____

   ____

   ____

2. The Wilders make almost everything they use, so why don't they make their own shoes? ____________

   ____

   ____

3. Where is the Academy located? Why don't the children live at home while attending? ____________

   ____

   ____

4. What historic basis does Mother use for rebuking Eliza Jane's rude remark? ____________

   ____

   ____

5. Why does Royal want to be a storekeeper and not a farmer? ____________

   ____

Quotations

Dinner-time was gay. The cobbler told all the news, he praised Mother's cooking, and he told jokes till Father roared and Mother wiped her eyes. Then the cobbler asked Father what he should make first, and Father answered: "I guess you better begin with boots for Almanzo."

"It isn't the style to drink out of saucers any more," Eliza Jane said. "Nice people drink out of the cup."

Discussion Questions

1. *What is the significance of Father's announcement that Almanzo's boots should be made first?
2. This chapter describes some of the common tools used and the process of shoe making. Using the context of the story, try to answer the following questions: What is a *last*? What is a *vise*, and how is it used? What is an *awl*? What is a *rasp*? What does it mean to "bore a hole"?

Enrichment

Focus Passage – Dialogue:

When characters in a story talk to one another, it's called "dialogue." When writing dialogue, every time a new character speaks, a new paragraph is begun.

Carefully copy the dialogue between Mother and Eliza Jane on page 296, beginning with "It isn't the style ..." and ending with "... where saucers come from." Watch indentations and punctuation!

Reading Notes

timber trees or wooded land considered as a source of wood
bobsled a long sled made of two shorter sleds joined together, one behind the other
tongue the harnessing pole attached to the front end of an animal-drawn vehicle

Vocabulary

1. First Father **hewed** the bottoms of the runners flat and smooth... ______________________
2. ...clear around the **crook** of their turned-up front ends. ______________________
3. Into the holes he drove **stout** wooden pegs. ______________________
4. For the tongue he used an elm **sapling**,... ______________________
5. ...elm is tougher and more **pliable** than oak. ______________________

Comprehension Questions

1. Why does Almanzo want his very own bobsled? ______________________

____

____

2. Why does Father show Almanzo how to make the sled rather than make it for him? ____________

____

____

____

____

3. Why does Father use an elm sapling for the tongue? ______________________

____

____

____

4. Why does Almanzo want deep snow while it is storming? ______________________

____

____

Quotations

Snow was falling next morning when Almanzo rode with Father to the timber lot. Large feathery flakes made a veil over everything, and if you were alone and held your breath and listened, you could hear the soft, tiny sound of their falling.

The storm was rising. The falling snow whirled and the wind was crying with a lonely sound when Almanzo and Father carried the full milk-pails to the house that night.

Discussion Questions

1. Read the quotations above. What imagery does the author use to describe the snow? What is seen? What is heard? What is felt? To what are the snowflakes and the wind compared?
2. What specific kinds of trees are needed to build the bobsled?
3. Describe the little bobsled, using as many details as you can.

Enrichment

Dictation: Listen carefully as your teacher reads aloud. As she reads, write down what you hear. Pay close attention to indentation, spelling, capitalization and punctuation. When finished, compare your paragraph to the book and circle any errors.

Reading Notes

cud food regurgitated from the stomach to the mouth and chewed again

flail a manual threshing tool made up of a wooden handle with a shorter, free-swinging stick attached to its end

fanning-mill a machine used to blow and separate chaff from the grain

hopper a funnel-shaped container through which grain passes to a machine

Vocabulary

1. When Almanzo **latched** the door behind him… ________________
2. The cows stood in a row, placidly swinging their **tasseled** tails ________________
3. Father … **riveted** the ends together to make a leather loop. ________________
4. That's a lazy man's way to **thresh**. ________________
5. a cloud of **chaff** blew out its front ________________

Comprehension Questions

1. How do the barns stand undisturbed against the howling storm? ________________
2. According to Father, what is a lazy man's way to thresh grain? What is wrong with saving time?
3. What different crops are threshed and/or put through the fanning-mill? ________________
4. Describe how Almanzo feels while he spends time in the snug barns threshing and doing his chores. ________________

Quotations

"All it saves is time, son. And what good is time, with nothing to do?"

Who said this? ______________________ About what? ______________________

Almanzo had harrowed the fields, he had helped in the harvest, and now he was threshing. He helped to feed the patient cows, and the horses eagerly whinnying over the bars of their stalls, and the hungrily bleating sheep, and the grunting pigs. And he felt like saying to them all: "You can depend on me. I'm big enough to take care of you all."

Discussion Questions

1. Describe how Father and Almanzo thresh grain. How is the flail used?
2. What is Almanzo likely to become when he grows up? What evidence supports your idea?
3. Is there a place that feels completely comfortable and familiar to you? Why?

Enrichment

Expressions to Know: Briefly explain what each of the following phrases means.

1. haste makes waste ______________________
2. What good is time with nothing to do? ______________________
3. sit and twiddle your thumbs ______________________
4. peck-measure ______________________
5. You can depend on me. ______________________

Reading Notes

horehound	a type of candy, made from a plant in the mint family
cravat	a band of fabric worn around the neck as a tie
dast	a slang term for "dare"

Vocabulary

1. Bad boys found nothing but **switches** in their stockings… ______
2. he could hardly stand the **strain**. ______
3. He had to **scour** the steel knives and forks… ______
4. Almanzo's insides **quaked**. ______
5. Spoons … **gouged** deep into the mashed potatoes… ______

Comprehension Questions

1. What does the threat of a switch have to do with Almanzo's good behavior? ______
2. Why did Almanzo quake when he heard Mother's comment that he might spill the stove blacking? ______
3. Describe Christmas morning. Why does Father say to look at the clock? ______
4. What does Frank dare Almanzo to do? What happens? ______

Quotations

For a long time it seemed that Christmas would never come. On Christmas, Uncle Andrew and Aunt Delia, Uncle Wesley and Aunt Lindy, and all the cousins were coming to dinner. It would be the best dinner of the whole year. And a good boy might get something in his stocking.

"I guess I'd do it if I wanted to, if I was you. I guess your father wouldn't know."

Who said this? ______________________ About what? ______________________

Discussion Questions

1. What gifts does Almanzo receive? Why are these "practical" gifts so important to him?
2. Why is anticipation sometimes both wonderful and difficult at the same time?
3. Name some of the foods Mother serves at Christmas dinner. Why does Almanzo think the adults are heartless?
4. Christmas traditions can vary from family to family as well as from culture to culture. Compare and contrast the Wilders' Christmas traditions with those of your own family.

Enrichment

Focus Passage: Copy the last full paragraph on page 315 ("But Almanzo was already …"). Spelling, punctuation, and capitalization should be perfect.

Reading Notes

skid	timber used as a support or track for rolling heavy objects
cant-poles	long, sharp poles with a free-swinging iron hook at one end
topsy-turvy, pell-mell	both expressions mean a state of utter disorder; confusion
corded	cut to the same length and stacked

Vocabulary

1. he fed them carrots and talked to them **soothingly**. ____________________
2. You **spoil** a team if you let them see-saw. ____________________
3. They snorted and **floundered** and plunged ____________________
4. They snorted and floundered and **plunged** ____________________
5. But can you **figure**? ____________________

Comprehension Questions

1. Father's French neighbors come to help with the wood hauling. What other things (in previous chapters) have they helped the Wilders do? ____________________

   ____

2. What is Almanzo's accident? How does his father react? ____________________

   ____

   ____

   ____

3. What is Almanzo's reaction to his mother's suggestion that he stop work after his accident? ______

   ____

4. Almanzo has been taught to be patient and gentle with his oxen. What is an example of how his patience helps when things go wrong? ____________________

   ____

   ____

5. What is Almanzo's chief motivation for studying hard at arithmetic? ____________________

   ____

Quotations

"Accidents will happen, son. Take more care next time. Men must look out for themselves in the timber."

Who said this? ______________________________ To whom? ______________________________

He had to sit down and rest a minute. But he got up, and he petted Star and Bright and spoke to them encouragingly. He took an apple away from Pierre and broke it in two and gave it to the little steers. When they had eaten it, he cracked his whip and cheerfully shouted: "Giddap!"

To whom does this refer? ______________________

Discussion Questions

1. Explain how logs are lifted onto the bobsleds to be hauled back to the farm.
2. What does Father do the first time he notices Almanzo struggling with his oxen in the ditch? What does he do the second time it happens? Why?

Enrichment

Sequencing: It is important, and often necessary, to remember the order of events in a story. Put the following events in order by numbering them from 1 to 8.

_____ "Well, well, no bones broken!" Father said cheerfully.

_____ Driving his own sled and oxen, Almanzo followed his father into the woods.

_____ A log fell on Almanzo and smashed him into the snow.

_____ Almanzo stayed patient with his team regardless of their mistakes.

_____ Almanzo did not have to go to school because it was time to haul wood.

_____ Once hauling was finished, Almanzo returned to school.

_____ Almanzo searched for three straight poles to use for skids.

_____ Star and Bright could not move because the sled was too heavily loaded.

Reading Notes

pocketbook	a pocket-sized case used to hold money and papers; a billfold
banknote	a note, promising to pay a sum on demand; accepted as money
liveryman	someone who works in a stable that boards horses

Vocabulary

1. You measly **skinflint**! ______
2. Almanzo was so excited he **stammered**. ______
3. The bills were **clutched** tight in his hand. ______
4. And I figure the boy's **entitled** to it. ______
5. And I'm much **obliged** to you, Paddock ______

Comprehension Questions

1. Why does Father sell some of his hay? Briefly explain how it is baled. ______
2. To what is Father referring when he tells Almanzo, "Learning is best put into practice"? ______
3. What three questions does Father ask himself about the owner of the pocketbook? Who is the owner? ______
4. How does Almanzo bargain with the liveryman? ______
5. Why does Father initially object to Almanzo taking the money? ______

Quotations

"Learning is best put into practice. What say you ride to town with me tomorrow, and sell that load of hay?"

Who said this? ______________________ To whom? ______________________

Then he breathed a long sigh of relief, and said, "Well, this durn boy didn't steal any of it."

Who said this? ______________________ About whom? ______________________

Discussion Questions

1. What does Father mean when he says, "Many a good beginning makes a bad ending"?
2. Mr. Case says, "I'd rather have a nimble sixpence than a slow shilling." What are sixpence and shillings? Explain the statement.
3. *What does Almanzo mean when he gives the nickel back and says, "I can't change it."? Why is he so angry at Mr. Thompson?
4. Reread the last two paragraphs of the chapter. What is Almanzo already planning to do with his money? Why is this exciting for the reader? How does the last line increase your desire to read on to the next chapter?

Enrichment

Learn More: Using the context of the story, study to find the definition of each of the words below. Then match the term to its correct definition.

1. _____ a rotating spindle or shaft		a. hewed
2. _____ a heavy, long-handled hammer used to pound stakes		b. maul
3. _____ a flexible twig used to bind things together		c. withe
4. _____ curved pieces of a harness around the neck of a draft animal		d. hay-baler
5. _____ a person or machine that forms hay into bales		e. railroad press
6. _____ a long pole attached to a pivot		f. capstan
7. _____ cut or shaped with an ax		g. sweep
8. _____ a box-shaped machine used for baling hay		h. hames

Reading Notes

wheelwright	one who builds and repairs wheels
"a piece of your mind"	an opinion; usually said with strong feeling or emotion
"at the beck and call of every Tom, Dick, and Harry"	always available at others' request and convenience

Vocabulary

1. It's a good **opening** for a smart young fellow. ____________________
2. **Apprentice** him to me, and I'll treat the boy right. ____________________
3. curled away from the **keen** edges of the planes. ____________________
4. How does Mr. Paddock make his money, if it isn't **catering** to us? ____________________
5. **Truckling** to other people for his living ____________________

Comprehension Questions

1. What does Mr. Paddock discuss with Father? What does Almanzo like about Mr. Paddock's work?

   ____

   ____

   ____

2. Why does Mother think moving to town is a step down from being a farmer? ____________________

   ____

   ____

3. What does Almanzo dislike about the life of Mr. Paddock? ____________________

   ____

4. What does Almanzo want more than anything in the world? How does he decide this? ____________________

   ____

   ____

   ____

5. What is Almanzo's request that convinces Father of his desire to be a farmer? ____________________

   ____

Quotations

"You ever think of making a wheelwright out of him?"

Who said this? ______________________ About whom? ______________________

"A farmer depends on himself, and the land and the weather. If you're a farmer, you raise what you eat, you raise what you wear, and you keep warm with wood out of your own timber. You work hard, but you work as you please, and no man can tell you to go or come. You'll be free and independent, son, on a farm."

Who said this? ______________________ To whom? ______________________

Discussion Questions

1. *Compare and contrast Mother's and Father's hopes for Almanzo's future.
2. *Father is fair and honest with Almanzo about his options. How does he explain city life? How does he explain farm life?
3. After reading *Farmer Boy*, what do you find appealing about farm life?

Enrichment

Poetry Connection: "The Happy Farmer" summarizes the joys of farming in a beautifully poetic way.

Do the following:

1. Find the poem "The Happy Farmer" in the Appendix.
2. Read it through several times.
3. Discuss the meanings of the words, the aspects of poetry, and its message.
4. Copy it carefully and precisely.
5. Then memorize it, so that you may enjoy it in the future, whenever you wish.

Character: Character means <u>who</u> is in the story.

Create one sentence describing a change you observed in Almanzo since the beginning of the book.

____

____

Setting: Setting means the <u>time</u> and <u>place</u> in which the story happens.

1. Write one sentence about a place in the story, other than the Wilders' farm. ____________________

   ____

   ____

2. Write one sentence describing what Almanzo saw in Mr. Paddock's shop. Strong imagery (sights, sounds, smells) will improve your sentence. ____________________

   ____

   ____

Plot: Plot means <u>action</u> or <u>what happens</u> in the story.

Write about the plot related to Almanzo finding and returning Mr. Thompson's pocketbook. Summarize the action that takes place. Use plenty of detail.

____

____

____

____

____

____

____

____

____

____

____

Drawing Page

Illustrate a scene from your favorite chapter of *Farmer Boy*.
Write the chapter title above your picture.

Title goes here

Quiz 3 Review

Vocabulary

Write the letter of the vocabulary word on the line in front of its definition.

1. _______ serving	a. tapered
2. _______ grouped	b. pliable
3. _______ struggled helplessly	c. thresh
4. _______ has a right to	d. tasseled
5. _______ manners	e. trodden
6. _______ sharp	f. soothingly
7. _______ cape	g. stout
8. _______ to polish by scrubbing	h. clutched
9. _______ one who works for instruction	i. cloak
10. _______ pointed	j. scour
11. _______ stuttered	k. floundered
12. _______ bound at one end w/ loose threads	l. deportment
13. _______ scissors	m. entitled
14. _______ hard, outer covering of grain	n. apprentice
15. _______ to separate grain from chaff	o. clustered
16. _______ trampled; worn down	p. stammered
17. _______ in a calming manner	q. hewed
18. _______ strong	r. obliged
19. _______ held tightly	s. shears
20. _______ chopped; carved	t. quaked
21. _______ lean	u. chaff
22. _______ thankful	v. gaunt
23. _______ flexible	w. keen
24. _______ to remove outer leaves	x. catering
25. _______ shook violently	y. husk

Short Answer

Answer the following questions in complete sentences.

1. What does the threat of a switch have to do with Almanzo's good behavior before Christmas? ____

2. Give an example of how Almanzo has learned to use patience and gentleness in training his oxen.

3. Why is Almanzo so angry with Mr. Thompson? ____

4. Explain the difference between Mother's and Father's hopes for Almanzo's future. ____

5. What does Almanzo want more than anything in the world? How does he decide this? ____

Vocabulary Crosswords

Using the definitions below, choose the vocabulary word from the word bank to fit the puzzle.

Word Bank

placidly	sternly	shears	pliable	obliged
tapered	scour	inquiry	chaff	balk
sleek	briskly	impudently	hatchet	drowsy

Across:

1. to polish by scrubbing
2. to stop short and refuse to go on
4. question
5. pointed
7. smooth; slick
8. calmly; peacefully
12. firmly; severely
13. thankful

Down:

1. scissors
2. quickly; with spirit
3. disrespectfully
6. flexible
9. hard, outer covering of grain
10. small, short-handled ax
11. sleepy

Vocabulary Crosswords

Using the definitions below, choose the vocabulary word from the word bank to fit the puzzle.

Word Bank

swathes	hustle	clutched	askew	term
trodden	aromatic	rousing	shrewd	dawdle
apprentice	soothingly	dappled	gritty	trudged

Across:

1. walked with heavy feet
7. bent to one side
9. sandy
11. to waste time; to be slow
13. held tightly
14. scented
15. crafty; clever

Down:

2. waking
3. spotted
4. sections, rows
5. one who works in return for instruction
6. grading period; semester
8. trampled; worn down
10. in a calming manner
12. hurry

Character Identification

Using the name bank, match each name to a description and write the name on the line.

Mother	Mr. Thompson	Frank	Nick Brown	Mr. Paddock
Mr. Corse	Father	Almanzo	Eliza Jane	horse-buyer

1. ______________________ disobedient; dares Almanzo to do things
2. ______________________ his word is as good as his bond
3. ______________________ bossy; always knows what is best to do
4. ______________________ gentle and patient and never whips little boys
5. ______________________ about nine years old; loves farming
6. ______________________ short and plump and pretty
7. ______________________ a wheelwright; owner of the wagon shop
8. ______________________ suspicious of banks and selfish with his money
9. ______________________ a jolly, fat man who tells stories and sings songs
10. ______________________ wears city clothes, has black eyes, and a waxed mustache

Who Said That?

Using the name bank at the top of the page, match each name to a quotation and write the name on the line.

1. ______________________ "I guess I know how to handle my own calves."
2. ______________________ "It isn't the style to drink out of saucers anymore."
3. ______________________ "You're a good milker, son."
4. ______________________ "You ever think of making a wheelwright out of him?"
5. ______________________ "Stay in at recess and learn it."
6. ______________________ "I guess I'd do it if I wanted to, if I was you."
7. ______________________ "Well, this durn boy didn't steal any of it."
8. ______________________ "All right, two hundred it is. I'll lose money by it, but here you are."
9. ______________________ "My butter speaks for itself."
10. ______________________ "I'll tell story for story and sing song for song …"

Multiple Choice

Choose the best answer for each question.

1. Why does Almanzo anxiously await the dark of the moon in May?
   a. It is time to plant crops, and he loves working in the fields with Father.
   b. It becomes warmer and he can stay outdoors longer.
   c. He can stay home from school and plant pumpkins.

2. Why does Almanzo's teacher stay with the Wilder family at their home?
   a. He is poor and has nowhere else to go.
   b. He likes their family the best of all the other families.
   c. Each family boards the teacher for two weeks, and it is the Wilders' turn.

3. Why don't the Wilders make their own shoes?
   a. They don't have the right quality of animal hide for shoes.
   b. Cobblers' work is highly skilled and requires special equipment.
   c. They are too busy farming and don't have time to make shoes.

4. On Independence Day, when Almanzo wants a nickel, why does Father ask him about potatoes?
   a. He wants him to understand how much work goes into earning money and to value it.
   b. Father wants to convince Almanzo not to buy lemonade.
   c. Father wants to impress his adult friend with Almanzo's farming knowledge.

5. What gifts does Almanzo receive from his parents for his birthday? **Both** must be true!
   a. a sled and warm, woolen mittens
   b. a small yoke for his ox calves and a sled
   c. a jack-knife and a yoke for his oxen

6. Why does Father show Almanzo how to make the sled rather than just make it all for him?
   a. Father wants him to learn the skills by doing it himself, and he knows that will also teach him to more deeply appreciate and take care of the sled.
   b. Father doesn't have the time to make it for him; Almanzo has to help or it won't get done.
   c. He wants Almanzo to be able to fix his sled by himself if it is ever broken.

7. What does Mr. Paddock discuss with Father?
   a. Mr. Paddock has no sons of his own and wants Almanzo to work for him as an apprentice.
   b. Mr. Paddock wants to ask Father's permission to recommend Almanzo to another farmer for a job.
   c. Mr. Paddock admires Almanzo's honesty and wants to say so to Father.

8. What does Almanzo like **best** about Saturdays, and what does he like **least**? **Both** must be true!
   a. no school / knowing that tomorrow he has to sit still all day
   b. baking day / taking a bath
   c. fewer chores on Saturday / taking a bath

9. Why is Father in a hurry to harvest the potatoes?
   a. He has so much other work to do for harvesting that is more important to get done.
   b. There is a threat of frost which will kill the potato crop.
   c. The family has no potatoes left to eat and they depend on them for food.

10. What makes Almanzo feel grown-up and important at the fair?
   a. He is allowed to leave his parents and spend time playing with his cousin.
   b. He knows the names of all the different types of horses, cows, and sheep at the fair.
   c. He feels important talking about horses with Father.

Short Answer

Answer the questions below in complete sentences.

1. Throughout most of the book, Father does not trust Almanzo around the colts. What does he fear will happen? ____

2. Name and *briefly* describe TWO different salesmen that visit the Wilder farm. __________________

3. The Wilders grow or make much of what they use for everyday living. List three things they need on a regular basis that they produce themselves on their farm. __________________________

4. Choose one of the following "lessons" that Almanzo learns as a child, and give an example from the book of how he learned or used this lesson. *(patience, the value of money, telling the truth)*

5. What does Father do at the end of the book that proves he thinks Almanzo is growing up? ______

______

______

Paragraph

Answer the question below in 3-5 complete sentences.

Describe a farmer based on what you know after reading *Farmer Boy.*

______

______

______

______

______

______

______

______

______

______

Appendix

Laura Ingalls Wilder

Laura Ingalls Wilder, author of the *Little House* series, was born February 7, 1867. She was the second of five children, having three surviving sisters and one brother who died in infancy. She was born near Pepin, Wisconsin, and her life there served as the basis for her book *Little House in the Big Woods.*

The Ingalls Family: seated from left Caroline (Laura's mother), Charles (Laura's father), Mary. Standing from left Carrie, Laura, Grace.

In Laura's early childhood, her father moved the family to Indian territory in Kansas, hoping to establish a homestead. This period of her life is recounted in *Little House on the Prairie*. In the following years, Pa Ingalls moved his family to Minnesota, Iowa, back to Minnesota, and finally to South Dakota where he, his wife, and daughter Mary remained for the rest of their lives.

Once the family was settled in DeSmet, South Dakota, Laura was able to attend school and eventually met her future husband, Almanzo Wilder. She accepted a teaching position at the age of 15, teaching in various one-room schools and continuing her own education as well. By her own admission, she never really enjoyed teaching, but did so to aid her family financially.

On August 28, 1885, Laura Ingalls and "Manly" Wilder were married, at which time Laura quit teaching. Despite a promising beginning, she and Almanzo (see left) experienced many difficulties during their life together, both physically and financially. Through hard work, determination, and some outside help, they were able to eventually establish a prosperous farm in Mansfield, Missouri, called Rocky Ridge Farm. They remained at this farm until their deaths, Almanzo in 1949 at the age of ninety-two, and Laura in 1957 at the age of ninety.

A 19th Century Primer

Many different kinds of primers have been published and used throughout the years in the United States. Perhaps the two best known are The New England Primer and McGuffey Readers.

The New England Primer

Nightingales sing
In time of spring.

The sturdy Oak, it was the tree,
That saved his royal majesty.

Peter denies
His Lord, and cries.

Queen Esther comes in royal state,
To save the Jews from dismal fate.

Rachel doth mourn
For her first born.

Samuel anoints
Whom God appoints.

This teaching text was first published between 1687 and 1690 by a man named Benjamin Harris. It was the first reading primer to be published in the American Colonies and became the most widely used textbook in the early days of America. It consisted of the alphabet, vowels, consonants, and various two-to-six letter syllables. Reading was taught primarily through the use of short religious prayers and poetry, wood cut pictures, and moral lessons. Some versions of this text also included a short catechism. Respect for one's parents, sin, and salvation were common themes.

During this early period of history, other, more secular, primers were also written but did not stay in use for long. The alphabet, however, remained the common systematic means of introducing reading and spelling to young children.

McGuffey Readers

These enduring classics were originally written by William Holmes McGuffey and first published in 1836-1837. They were written as a set of four readers, each one progressing in difficulty from the previous. They used word repetition as a learning tool.

The first Reader used the phonics method and focused on identifying letters, simple words, and writing practice (done on a slate). Once a child had mastered these beginning skills of reading, he moved into the second Reader. This taught him to understand the meaning of sentences and provided vivid stories and lessons that could be easily remembered. The third Reader taught advanced skills and definitions of words, while the fourth, and final, Reader aimed at the highest level of learning in the grammar school.

FIRST READER. 11

LESSON V.

Răb Ănn hăt cătch sēe

ē ch s

See Rab! See Ann!
See! Rab has the hat.
Can Ann catch Rab?

The earliest primers taught vocabulary through lists that were simply memorized. But McGuffey introduced a new style of presenting vocabulary, by using it within the context of a real story. He believed teachers should study the lessons with their students (instead of the student merely memorizing and reciting them) and encouraged reading aloud to the class. He also believed that asking questions was an important tool of teaching, and included questions at the end of each lesson.

The content of the earliest McGuffey Readers offered a curriculum rich in religious beliefs and manners. But as with the New England primers before, revised editions did not contain the same forthright values of salvation and piety. The content of the Readers became more focused on simply being a good person and treating others well. However, McGuffey himself neither wrote these revisions nor approved their content.

McGuffey Readers have declined in use over the years, but have not entirely disappeared. They are still in use today, especially within the homeschool movement.

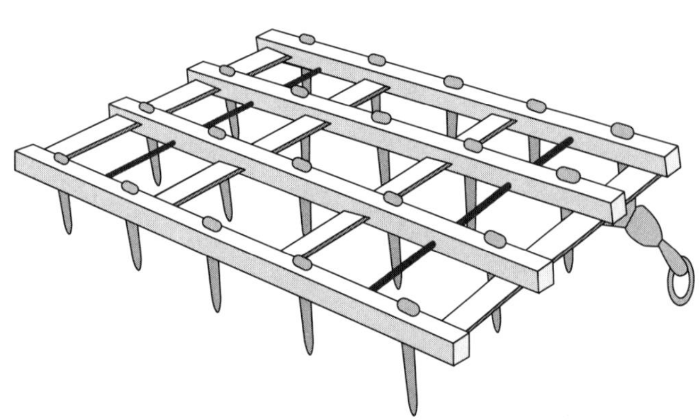

harrow:

A harrow was used for the preparation of the soil before planting. It served to smooth out rough, clumpy soil to ensure that crops could be planted evenly. Iron spikes were attached to a wooden frame and the frame was then pulled behind horses. The harrow pictured here was used in areas that were already free of large obstacles such as tree stumps.

plow:

During the 1800's, a plow was the most important piece of farming equipment. It was used to break up and turn the soil before planting a crop. With a plow such as the one pictured here, a whole day was needed to plow only 1-2 acres of land! Plows were expensive, and most farmers could not afford to own one. Therefore, farmers who were fortunate enough to own a plow often loaned it to their surrounding neighbors in exchange for labor or goods.

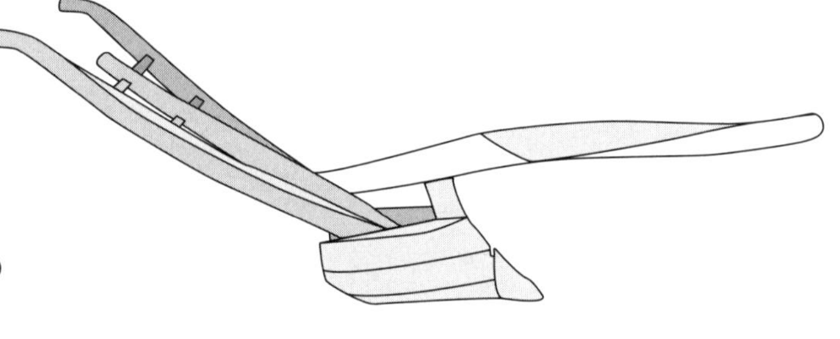

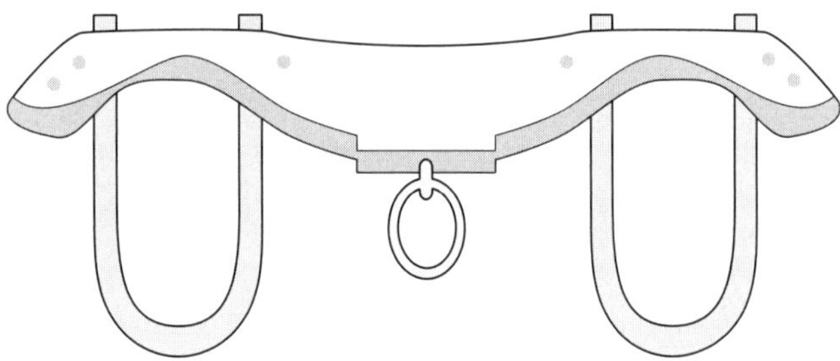

yoke:

This is a straight yoke, the most common kind used for oxen. The large wooden bar was fitted on the back of the oxen's necks while the U-shaped bows were fitted under the neck and were attached with iron pins. A plow or wagon could be attached to the large iron ring in the middle of the yoke.

flail:

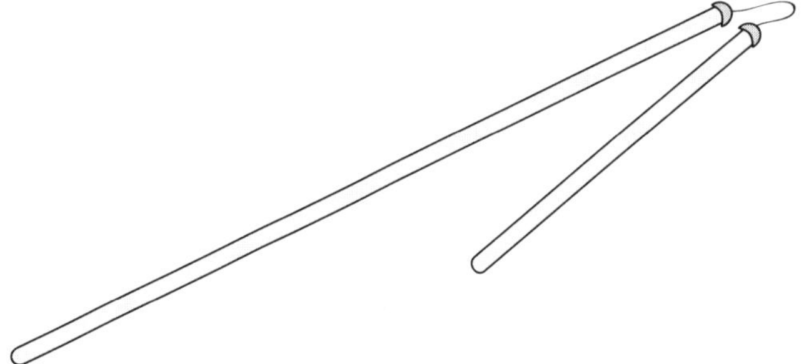

This was a tool used for threshing grain. It was made of a long wooden handle attached with leather loops to a shorter stick. The grain was laid out on the floor of a barn and the thresher would swing the handle of the flail in a circular motion—first down, back, then around and over the head. As it continued around and down, the shorter stick would swing freely, striking the grain. As it was beaten, the kernels of grain would separate from the husk and fall through the straw to the floor. The straw was then carefully lifted, and the grain was collected and stored.

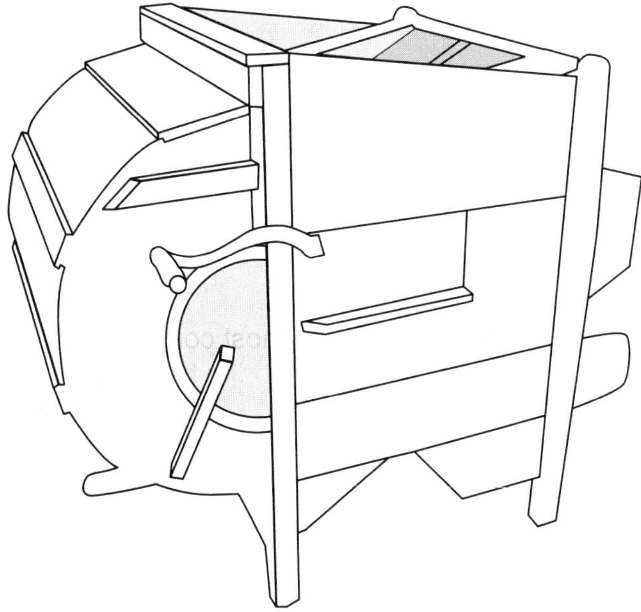

fanning-mill:

This tool was used to separate wheat grain from the chaff (garbage). The harvested grain was shoveled into the "hopper" on top while the handle was turned. As the fans worked inside the mill, chaff was blown out the front of the machine. The kernels of clean wheat came out and were collected on another side.

scythe:

A scythe was used primarily for cutting grass or reaping crops. In Almanzo's day, they were usually made from wood, having a straight shaft with a short grip and a curved metal blade. Mowing with a scythe is done by holding the top handle with the left hand and the central grip in the right hand. The arms remain straight and the blade stays parallel and close to the ground. As a person cuts, the body twists to the left in a steady rhythm. As the grain is cut, it falls in rows, called swathes, on the ground, to be gathered later.

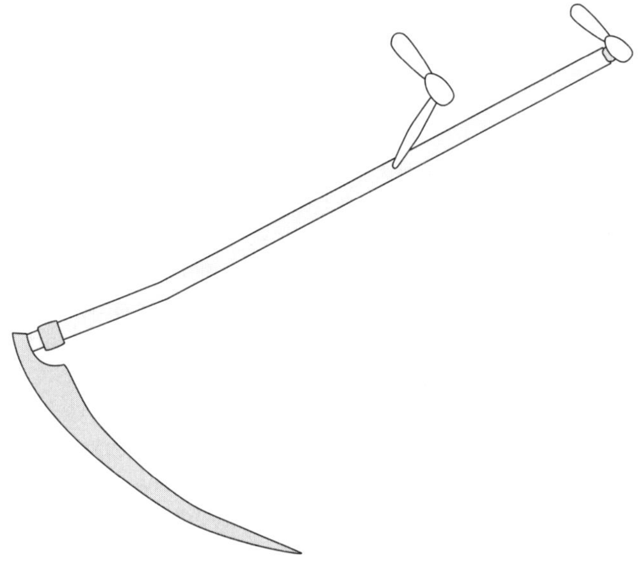

hay press:

The hay press (or as the book indicates, also known as a "railroad press") was an early form of the hay-baler and was used to bundle hay in order to make it easier for transport. They came into use around the middle of the 1800's, but were not used regularly by the average farmer until the 1870's. The fact that the Wilders used one speaks of their wealth and progressive farming practices. It was a stationary machine powered by a horse. The box chamber was filled with hay, and as the horse walked in a circular motion, it set in action gears and a chain drive that compressed the hay tightly. It was then manually tied together with twine, wire, or, as in the book, ash-withes, which were strips of pliable tree bark.

A man's "waist."

A woman's "hoop skirt."

A woman's "basque."

Birds' Nest Pudding

Brown sugar baked in green apples, nested in a pastry crust
(as referred to in *Farmer Boy*, "Filling the Ice-House")

Ingredients:

6	green apples; tart, peeled, cored
1	cup brown sugar
¼ tsp	nutmeg
3	egg whites
3	egg yolks
1 cup	whole milk
1 tsp	maple flavoring

1 cup	flour
1 tsp	cream of tartar
½ tsp	baking powder
½ tsp	salt

Sweetened Cream:

½ cup	powdered sugar
¼ tsp	nutmeg
1 pint	heavy whipping cream

Directions:

1. **Preheat oven** to 350° F. Prepare a buttered 2-quart baking dish.
2. **Prepare the apples**: Place apples in baking dish. Fill each apple with brown sugar, pressing slightly. Save any unused sugar. Sprinkle nutmeg over the apples. Place dish in oven to begin baking as batter is prepared.
3. **Prepare the batter**: Beat the egg whites until stiff. In a separate bowl, beat the egg yolks until they change color. Add milk and maple flavoring to the yolks. In another separate bowl, mix the flour, cream of tartar, baking powder, salt, and the remaining brown sugar until well blended. Pour the flour mixture all together into the yolk mixture, stirring until blended. Fold the beaten egg whites into the blended flour and yolks. This batter will be thin.
4. **Combine apples and batter**: Remove apples from oven and pour batter into the baking dish, over and around the apples evenly. Return the dish to the oven and bake another 45 to 60 minutes.
5. **Prepare the cream**: Stir powdered sugar and nutmeg into the heavy cream.
6. Remove dish from oven when crust is lightly browned. Before it falls, quickly and carefully turn each apple along with some surrounding crust onto a plate, so the apple is nested in the crust. Top with sweetened cream.

The Hayloft

Through all the pleasant meadow-side
The grass grew shoulder-high,
Till the shining scythes went far and wide
And cut it down to dry.

These green and sweetly smelling crops
They led in wagons home;
And they piled them here in mountain tops
For mountaineers to roam.

Here is Mount Clear, Mount Rusty-Nail,
Mount Eagle and Mount High;—
The mice that in these mountains dwell,
No happier are than I!

O what a joy to clamber there,
O what a place for play,
With the sweet, the dim, the dusty air,
The happy hills of hay!

The Happy Farmer

Let the mighty and great
Roll in splendor and state,
I envy them not, I declare it.
I eat my own lamb,
My own chicken and ham;
I shear my own sheep and I wear it.

I have lawns and green bowers,
Fresh fruits and fine flowers,
The lark is my bright morning charmer.
So God bless the plow
In the future as now—
A health and long life to the farmer.